CANVA
SIMPLIFIED

"Unlocking Creativity: A
Simplified Guide to Canva
Mastery"

VINCENT SIMS

Copyright ©

Dedication

"To all aspiring creators, may your artistic journey be illuminated by the simplicity and power of Canva. This book is dedicated to the limitless possibilities within each canvas, waiting to be brought to life."

Table of Contents

Acknowledgments

"I extend my heartfelt gratitude to the team at Canva for crafting a tool that has revolutionized the way we express creativity. Special thanks to the countless users whose feedback and enthusiasm have inspired this simplified guide. To my mentors, friends, and family – your unwavering support has been my greatest source of motivation. This book is a collective effort, and I am grateful for each person who played a role in its creation."

Preface

In the age of digital expression, creativity knows no bounds. As the canvas evolves from the traditional to the digital realm, Canva emerges as a beacon of simplicity and empowerment. 'Canva Simplified' is not just a guide; it is an invitation to explore the seamless fusion of imagination and technology.

This book is born out of a passion for making the creative process accessible to all. Whether you're a seasoned designer or a newcomer to the world of graphic design, the pages ahead are crafted to demystify Canva's potential. Through step-by-step instructions, practical tips, and creative insights, we embark on a journey to harness the full spectrum of Canvas capabilities.

As we navigate the landscape of digital design, remember that the canvas is not just a space; it's a playground of possibilities. 'Canva Simplified' is your compass, designed to empower your creativity and simplify your artistic endeavors.

Let the journey begin.

[VINCENT SIMS]"

Chapter 1.

Introduction to Canva

- 1.1 Understanding Canvas Interface

Canva, a revolutionary online design platform, has redefined the way individuals and businesses approach graphic design. With its user-friendly interface and a vast array of design tools, Canva empowers both professionals and amateurs to create visually stunning content effortlessly.

At the heart of Canva's appeal lies its intuitive interface, designed for simplicity without compromising on functionality. Let's delve into key aspects:

Canva: The canva is your digital workspace, where the magic happens. It's akin to a blank sheet of paper waiting to be transformed into a masterpiece. Understand the canvas dimensions, customize it to your needs, and embrace the infinite possibilities it offers.

Toolbar: Located on the left, the toolbar is your creative arsenal.

From text and elements to backgrounds and uploads, each tool serves a unique purpose. Familiarize yourself with these instruments to seamlessly bring your ideas to life.

Design Tabs: Canva design tabs streamline your creative process. Whether it's social media graphics, presentations, posters, or other projects, choose the relevant tab to access pre-sized templates tailored for specific purposes.

Sidebar: The right sidebar is a treasure trove of options. It houses templates, uploads, and designs, allowing you to effortlessly manage your projects. Explore this space to organize, edit, and enhance your creations.

Menu Bar: Located at the top, the menu bar provides additional functionalities. From file management to collaboration tools, this bar is your command center for executing actions beyond the canvas.

Navigating the Canvas interface is the first step toward mastering this dynamic platform. As we embark on this journey of simplifying Canva, keep these foundational elements in mind – they are the building blocks of your design adventures. So, let's unravel the creative potential within the Canva interface and unleash your artistic vision.

- 1.2 Navigating Canvas Tools

Unlocking the full potential of Canva requires a grasp of its diverse toolkit. Each tool serves a unique purpose, equipping you with the means to transform your creative visions into reality. Let's navigate through the essential tools that form the backbone of the Canva experience:

1. Text Tool:

Express yourself with words using the Text tool. Add headings, subheadings, or body text to your design. Customize fonts, sizes, colors, and styles to make your text visually compelling.

2. Elements:

The Elements tool provides a library of shapes, icons, and illustrations. Enhance your design by dragging and dropping elements onto the canvas. Resize, rotate and customize them to suit your creative vision.

3. Uploads:

Bring your personal touch to designs by uploading images, logos, or other graphics. The Uploads tool allows you to seamlessly incorporate your visuals into Canva projects.

4. Background:

Set the tone for your design with the Background tool. Choose from Canva's extensive collection or upload your images to create the perfect backdrop for your project.

5. Templates:

Jumpstart your creativity with professionally designed templates. The Templates tool offers a wide range of layouts for various purposes, saving you time and ensuring a polished look for your designs.

6. Position and Arrange:

Effortlessly arrange elements on the canvas using the Position tool. Align, distribute, and layer objects to achieve the desired composition.

7. Group and Ungroup:

The Group and Ungroup tools allow you to organize multiple elements as a single unit or break them apart for individual editing. Streamline your design process and maintain control over every detail.

8. Effects:

Add flair to your designs with the Effects tool. Apply filters, adjust transparency, or add shadows to enhance the visual appeal of your creations.

9. Undo and Redo:

Mistakes happen, and that's okay. Canva's Undo and Redo tools become your safety net, allowing you to experiment fearlessly and revert changes with ease.

Mastering these essential tools will elevate your Canva experience, giving you the confidence to bring your ideas to life. Whether you're crafting social media graphics, presentations, or posters, navigate Canva's toolkit with creativity and precision. The canvas is yours—let the tools empower your artistic journey.

Chapter 2.

Design Basics

- 2.1 Color Theory and Canva

Color is a powerful language in design, capable of conveying emotions, setting moods, and influencing perceptions. Understanding color theory is essential for creating visually appealing and effective designs in Canva. Here's how you can leverage color theory principles within the Canva platform:

1. Color Wheel Basics:

Canva's color wheel is your guide to harmonious color combinations. Familiarize yourself with the primary colors (red, blue, yellow), secondary colors (orange, green, purple), and tertiary colors. The wheel helps you identify complementary, analogous, and triadic color schemes, allowing you to create visually balanced designs.

2. Color Palettes:
Canva offers pre-made color palettes or allows you to create custom ones. A palette simplifies your design process by ensuring consistency. Choose a dominant color for emphasis, secondary colors for supporting elements, and accent colors for highlights. Canva's

palettes make it easy to maintain a cohesive look across your projects.

3. Color Psychology:
Understand the psychological impact of colors to evoke specific emotions in your audience. For instance, warm colors like red and orange can convey energy and passion, while cool colors like blue and green evoke calmness and serenity. Utilize Canva's color options to align your designs with the emotional tone you want to convey.

4. Color Picker and HEX Codes:
Canva's Color Picker tool allows you to select precise shades using HEX codes. This feature is invaluable for

maintaining brand consistency or matching specific color requirements. Inputting HEX codes ensures that your color choices align with external branding guidelines.

5. Backgrounds and Overlays:
Experiment with background colors and overlays to create visual interest. Canva provides a range of options, allowing you to enhance your design's overall aesthetic. Balance the background color with the content to ensure readability and visual appeal.

6. Color Transparency:
Adjusting color transparency can add depth and subtlety to your designs. Canva's transparency

feature lets you control the opacity of elements, allowing for creative layering and blending of colors.

By integrating color theory principles into your Canva designs, you not only enhance the visual impact but also communicate more effectively. Whether you're designing social media graphics, presentations, or marketing materials, leverage Canva's intuitive tools to create a harmonious and visually captivating color palette. Let color theory be your guide as you paint your canvas with creativity and purpose.

- 2.2 Typography Tips for Beginners

Typography plays a pivotal role in design, influencing how information is perceived and communicated. Whether you're creating social media graphics, presentations, or any other content in Canva, here are some essential typography tips for beginners:

1. Font Selection:
Choose fonts that align with the message and tone of your design. Canva provides a vast library of fonts, including various styles from elegant scripts to modern sans-serifs. Ensure readability by

selecting fonts that complement each other.

2. Hierarchy Matters:
Establish a clear hierarchy in your text. Use different font sizes, weights, and styles to distinguish between headings, subheadings, and body text. This helps guide the viewer's eye and communicates the importance of each piece of information.

3. Consistency is Key:
Maintain consistency in your font choices throughout your design. Consistency enhances visual appeal and ensures a cohesive look. Stick to a limited number of fonts, typically

two to three, to avoid overwhelming the viewer.

4. Readability:
Prioritize readability by considering factors like font size, line spacing, and contrast. Aim for an easily readable font size, especially for body text. Ensure there's enough contrast between text and background to prevent eye strain.

5. Kerning and Tracking:
Adjust kerning (space between individual characters) and tracking (space between all characters) to achieve optimal spacing. Be mindful of legibility; too much or too little spacing can impact how easily the text is read.

6. Text Alignment:
Choose text alignment based on your design's aesthetic and purpose. Left-aligned text is commonly used for readability, while centered or right-aligned text can add a sense of style. Just be intentional in your choice.

7. Use of Italics and Bold:
Italicize or bold specific words or phrases to emphasize key points. However, use these styling elements sparingly to maintain balance and prevent visual clutter.

8. Contrast and Color:
Experiment with font color and contrast. Ensure there's enough

contrast between text and background for readability. Canva allows you to play with color options to create visually appealing and accessible text.

9. Pay Attention to Spacing:
Consider the spacing between lines (leading) and paragraphs. Optimal spacing contributes to the overall readability and aesthetic of your design.

10. Experiment and Iterate:
Don't be afraid to experiment with different font combinations and styles. Canva offers a live preview feature, allowing you to see changes in real time. Iterate until you find a

typography setup that best complements your design.

Typography is a nuanced art, and these tips serve as a starting point for beginners. As you explore Canva's typography options, remember that practice and experimentation are key to mastering the art of text in the design.

Chapter 3

Creating Stunning Graphics

- 3.1 Mastering Canvas Elements

Canva provides a robust set of design elements that can elevate your graphics from ordinary to extraordinary. To master these elements and create stunning visuals, consider the following tips:

1. Utilize Templates:
Start your graphic journey with Canva's professionally designed

templates. These templates serve as a canvas for your creativity, offering a head start with layouts tailored for various purposes. Customize these templates to suit your vision and save valuable time.

2. Experiment with Text:
Text is a fundamental element that can significantly impact your design. Play with different fonts, sizes, and styles to find the right combination. Use the Text tool to convey your message effectively, ensuring readability and visual appeal.

3. Embrace Imagery:
Canva's vast library of images and illustrations provides endless possibilities. Incorporate visuals

that complement your message or theme. Pay attention to image quality and relevance to create a cohesive and impactful graphic.

4. Iconography and Elements:
Enhance your graphics with Canva's diverse collection of icons and elements. Whether you need arrows for emphasis or decorative elements for flair, these additions can elevate the overall aesthetic and guide the viewer's attention.

5. Color Harmony:
Master the use of colors to create a harmonious and visually pleasing composition. Leverage Canva's color tools, including palettes and the color wheel, to achieve balance and

evoke the desired emotions in your audience.

6. Background Magic:
Experiment with backgrounds to set the tone for your graphic. Canva offers a range of background options, from solid colors to intricate patterns. Ensure that your background complements the overall design without overshadowing key elements.

7. Layering Techniques:
Understanding how to effectively layer elements adds depth and sophistication to your graphics. Use the Arrange tool to position elements in the foreground or

background, creating a visually engaging composition.

8. Consistency in Design:
Maintain consistency in design elements throughout your graphic. Whether it's using a consistent color scheme, font style, or layout structure, coherence ensures a polished and professional look.

9. Smart Sizing:
Be mindful of dimensions, especially if you're creating graphics for specific platforms. Canva provides preset dimensions for social media, presentations, and more. Use these guidelines to ensure your graphics are optimized for their intended use.

10. Preview and Refine:
Take advantage of Canva's real-time preview feature to see how your design evolves. Regularly review and refine your graphics, paying attention to details like spacing, alignment, and overall visual balance.

Mastering Canva's elements involves a combination of creativity and technical skill. Whether you're crafting social media graphics, marketing materials, or presentations, these tips will guide you in creating stunning visuals that captivate your audience. Experiment, iterate, and let your creativity shine on the Canva canvas.

- 3.2 Incorporating Photos and Illustrations

Adding compelling visuals to your designs in Canva can breathe life into your creations, making them more engaging and memorable. Here are tips on effectively incorporating photos and illustrations:

1. Quality Matters:
Select high-quality images and illustrations. Whether sourced from Canva's extensive library or your uploads, crisp and clear visuals enhance the overall professionalism of your design.

2. Relevant Imagery:

Ensure that your chosen visuals align with the message or theme of your design. Whether it's a presentation slide, social media post, or marketing material, relevance contributes to the overall impact.

3. Layering Techniques:

Experiment with layering photos and illustrations to create depth and visual interest. Canva's Arrange tool allows you to bring elements forward or send them to the back, facilitating effective layering.

4. Blend Modes:

Explore different blend modes to seamlessly integrate photos and illustrations. Blend modes alter how layers interact, offering creative possibilities such as overlays, soft light effects, and more.

5. Customization Options:
Canva provides customization options for both photos and illustrations. Adjust the transparency of an image, crop it to fit your design, or modify colors to create a cohesive look.

6. Consistent Style:
Maintain a consistent style throughout your design. If you're combining photos and illustrations, ensure that they share a similar aesthetic. Consistency enhances visual harmony.

7. Text Integration:

Consider how text interacts with your visuals. Ensure that text is legible against the chosen background, and use text overlays or transparent boxes to create a polished and readable design.

8. Framing Elements:

Frame your visuals using shapes or borders to add structure and emphasis. Canva offers a variety of frames that can enhance the overall presentation of your photos and illustrations.

9. Embrace Negative Space:

Don't overcrowd your design. Embrace negative space to give your visuals room to breathe. This not only improves clarity but also adds a sense of elegance to your composition.

10. Preview and Adjust:
Regularly preview your design to evaluate how photos and illustrations work together. Make adjustments as needed, ensuring that each element contributes to the overall impact of your graphic.

Incorporating photos and illustrations in Canva is a creative journey that allows you to transform ideas into visually captivating designs. Whether you're crafting a social media graphic, poster, or presentation, these tips will help you seamlessly integrate visuals, elevating the visual appeal and storytelling capacity of your work.

Chapter 4.

Advanced Techniques

- 4.1 Animations and Interactive Designs

Unlocking the full potential of Canva goes beyond static graphics – dive into the realm of animations and interactive designs to create dynamic and engaging content. Here are advanced techniques to master these features:

1. Animated Elements:
Explore Canva's library of animated elements. Add animated stickers,

GIFs, or icons to bring movement to your design. Consider the theme and purpose of your project, and use animations sparingly to enhance visual interest.

2. GIF Creation:

Transform static images into GIFs using Canva's animation tools. Choose a sequence of images, add them to your design, and animate them to create eye-catching GIFs. This is perfect for showcasing a process or adding a playful touch to your designs.

3. Transition Effects:

If you're creating presentations or interactive designs, leverage Canva's transition effects. Add smooth transitions between slides or elements to create a more polished and professional presentation.

4. Interactive Buttons:

For interactive designs, incorporate clickable buttons using Canva's interactive features. Link these buttons to external URLs, pages within your design, or anchor links for a seamless navigation experience.

5. Embedding Media:

Enhance interactivity by embedding media such as videos or audio clips directly into your Canva design. This is particularly useful for presentations, digital brochures, or online portfolios where multimedia elements can elevate the viewer's experience.

6. Scrollable Designs:

Create scrollable designs for interactive websites or presentations. Utilize the "scroll to" feature to guide users through different sections of your design, providing a narrative flow and a more engaging experience.

7. Hover Effects:

Add an interactive touch with hover effects. Canva allows you to apply hover effects to elements, changing their appearance when users hover over them. This subtle interaction can add a layer of sophistication to your design.

8. Collaborative Animation:

Collaborate with team members on animated designs. Canva's collaborative features enable multiple users to work on a design simultaneously, making it easier to create complex animations or interactive elements collaboratively.

9. Publish and Share:

After creating your animated or interactive design, use Canva's publishing options to share your work. Publish designs as interactive PDFs, or animated GIFs, or embed them on websites, ensuring your audience can experience your creations seamlessly.

10. Mobile Optimization:
Consider mobile responsiveness when designing interactive content. Test how your animations and interactive elements function on different devices to ensure a smooth user experience across various screen sizes.

Embrace these advanced techniques in Canva to take your designs to the next level. Whether you're crafting presentations, interactive infographics, or engaging social media content, animations, and interactive designs add a dynamic touch that captivates and delights your audience.

- 4.2 Collaborative Design in Canva

Canva empowers teams to break down barriers and collaborate seamlessly on design projects. Here's how you can leverage the collaborative features of Canva for a truly synergistic design process:

1. Shared Design Access:
Collaboration starts with easy access. Canva allows multiple users to simultaneously work on a design project. Invite team members, clients, or collaborators to access and contribute to the same design in real time.

2. Team Collaboration:

Create and join teams within Canva to streamline collaboration. Teams provide a centralized space for members to share designs, and assets, and collaborate efficiently. It's an ideal way to keep projects organized and accessible to everyone involved.

3. Commenting and Feedback:

Communication is key in collaborative design. Canva enables users to leave comments directly on designs, facilitating real-time feedback. Discuss design choices, suggest improvements, and keep the conversation within the context of the project.

4. Design Version History:

Avoid version control headaches with Canva's version history feature. Easily track changes, revert to previous versions, and maintain a clear timeline of the design's evolution. This ensures that everyone is on the same page and can access earlier iterations if needed.

5. Design Sharing and Publishing:

Collaborate beyond the platform by sharing designs with a simple link. Canva provides various sharing options, allowing collaborators to view, comment, or edit based on the permissions you grant. Publish designs directly to social media or embed them on websites for seamless sharing.

6. Design Templates for Consistency:
Create design templates that uphold brand consistency. Teams can use these templates as a foundation for various projects, ensuring a cohesive visual identity across different collateral. This is particularly beneficial for marketing teams, agencies, or organizations with standardized branding.

7. Role-Based Permissions:
Fine-tune collaboration by assigning role-based permissions. Control who can edit, comment, or view a design to maintain security and prevent

accidental changes. This feature is especially valuable for projects with different stakeholders or clients.

8. Presentations Mode:

Transform your design into an interactive presentation using Canva's presentations mode. Engage collaborators by guiding them through your design, providing insights, and fostering discussion in real time.

9. Remote Collaboration:

Facilitate remote collaboration effortlessly. Canva's cloud-based platform ensures that team members can access, edit, and contribute to designs from anywhere, breaking down geographical barriers and enabling global collaboration.

10. Export and Print Collaboration: Collaboration doesn't end with the digital realm. Canva allows seamless export options for print, ensuring that collaborative designs can transition smoothly from the screen to tangible materials like brochures, posters, or business cards.

In a world where collaboration is key, Canva's collaborative design features pave the way for efficient teamwork. Whether you're working on marketing campaigns, presentations, or branding materials, harness the power of collective creativity with Canva's collaborative design capabilities.

Chapter 5.

Branding with Canva

- 5.1 Designing Consistent Brand Assets

Building a strong brand identity involves consistency across all visual elements. Canva empowers businesses and individuals to create and maintain consistent brand assets effortlessly. Here's how you can utilize Canva for designing cohesive and impactful brand assets:

1. Brand Kit:

Start by establishing a Brand Kit within Canva. This feature allows you to store and access your brand's essential elements – logo, color palette, fonts, and any branded imagery. With these elements readily available, you ensure consistency in every design.

2. Custom Color Palette:

Define and save your brand's color palette in Canva. This ensures that every design adheres to the established brand colors. Canva's color palette feature allows you to easily access and apply your chosen colors across various design elements.

3. Consistent Fonts:

Select and save the fonts that represent your brand's personality. Canva allows you to set default fonts within your Brand Kit, ensuring that every design maintains the same typographic style. This consistency strengthens brand recognition.

4. Branded Templates:

Designing consistent assets becomes streamlined with branded templates. Create templates for social media posts, presentations, flyers, or any other collateral, incorporating your brand elements. This not only saves time but also ensures a cohesive visual identity.

5. Logo Integration:

Place your logo strategically in your designs. Canva's drag-and-drop functionality makes it easy to add your logo to templates or create watermarks. Consistent logo usage reinforces brand familiarity.

6. Custom Grids and Frames:

Maintain a consistent layout by utilizing custom grids and frames. Canva allows you to save your preferred layouts, ensuring that designs across different channels adhere to a unified structure, reinforcing brand aesthetics.

7. Watermarking:

Protect your brand assets by adding watermarks. Whether it's for presentations, proposals, or social media graphics, Canva enables you to overlay watermarks featuring your logo or brand elements, enhancing brand visibility.

8. Collaborative Branding:

Foster collaboration on brand assets by inviting team members to access the Brand Kit. This ensures that everyone involved in design projects has access to the latest brand assets, promoting consistency across the entire team.

9. Export Options for Print:
Maintain brand consistency even in printed materials. Canva's export options cater to various print requirements. Export designs for business cards, brochures, or banners while ensuring that your brand colors and logos are faithfully represented.

10. Social Media Branding:

Craft consistent visuals for your social media channels. Canva provides templates perfectly sized for different platforms. Customize these templates with your brand elements to maintain a cohesive social media presence.

Canva's user-friendly interface and robust features make it an invaluable tool for branding. By designing consistent brand assets, you not only establish a strong visual identity but also build trust and recognition among your audience. Elevate your brand with Canva's versatile design capabilities.

- 5.2 Using Canva for Social Media Branding

Social media has become a powerful platform for brand communication, and Canva offers a suite of tools to enhance your social media branding efforts. Here's a guide on leveraging Canva for a cohesive and visually appealing social media presence:

1. Consistent Visuals Across Platforms:
Establish brand consistency by using Canva to create uniform

visuals across all your social media platforms. Customize templates for each platform, ensuring that your brand colors, fonts, and logo are consistently represented.

2. Social Media Graphics Templates: Canva provides a variety of pre-designed templates tailored for different social media channels. Utilize these templates for posts, stories, cover photos, and more. Edit them to align with your brand guidelines, saving time and ensuring a polished look.

3. Branded Content Creation:

Craft eye-catching and branded content for your posts. Use Canva's intuitive design tools to incorporate your logo, color scheme, and typography into graphics. Custom graphics help your content stand out and contribute to a cohesive brand identity.

4. Personalized Imagery:

Ditch generic stock photos and create personalized imagery using Canva. Incorporate your brand colors, logo, or messaging into visuals to make your content uniquely yours. This not only strengthens brand recognition but also adds a personal touch to your social media presence.

5. Animated Social Media Posts:
Capture attention with animated posts. Canva allows you to animate graphics, making your social media feed more dynamic. Animate your logo, promotional graphics, or any visual elements to add a touch of creativity to your posts.

6. Story Highlights and Icons:
Enhance your Instagram profile with custom story highlights and icons. Canva enables you to design icons that align with your brand.

Maintain consistency by using a unified color scheme or style for your story highlights.

7. Instagram Stories and Reels:
Design engaging and on-brand Instagram Stories and Reels using Canva. Utilize Canva's library of elements, stickers, and animations to create visually compelling short-form content. Ensure that your brand elements are seamlessly integrated into these formats.

8. Social Media Campaign Assets:
For special promotions or campaigns, design branded assets

using Canva. Create banners, posters, or promotional graphics that align with your brand aesthetic. Consistent branding across campaign materials reinforces brand identity.

9. Collaboration on Social Media Designs:
Collaborate seamlessly with team members or clients on social media designs. Canva's collaborative features allow multiple contributors to work on the same design, ensuring everyone is aligned with the brand guidelines.

10. Analytics and Iteration:

Analyze the performance of your social media graphics using platform analytics. Based on insights, iterate and refine your designs for optimal engagement. Canva's real-time editing capabilities make it easy to implement changes and keep your social media visuals fresh.

Canva's versatility and user-friendly interface make it an invaluable tool for social media branding. Elevate your online presence, tell your brand story visually, and connect with your audience through consistent and visually appealing social media graphics.

Chapter 6

Practical Applications

- 6.1 Designing Marketing Materials

Canva emerges as a game-changer in the realm of marketing materials, offering a user-friendly platform equipped with powerful design tools. Here's how you can practically apply Canva to create stunning and effective marketing materials:

1. Eye-Catching Flyers:
Craft attention-grabbing flyers for events, promotions, or product

launches. Canva provides ready-made templates that you can customize with your brand elements. From vibrant colors to compelling imagery, design flyers that captivate your audience.

2. Striking Posters:
Design visually striking posters to promote your brand or events. Canva's extensive library of elements, fonts, and templates ensures that your posters align with your brand's aesthetic. Create promotional materials that leave a lasting impression.

3. Professional Business Cards:
Impress clients and contacts with professionally designed business

cards. Canva offers customizable business card templates, allowing you to incorporate your logo, brand colors, and contact information seamlessly. Design a card that reflects the essence of your brand.

4. Compelling Brochures:
Design informative and visually appealing brochures with Canva. Utilize the platform's tools to create multi-page brochures that showcase your products or services. Maintain a consistent design language across all pages for a cohesive look.

5. Engaging Social Media Ads:
Elevate your social media advertising game with Canva. Design captivating visuals for

Facebook, Instagram, or Twitter ads. Leverage Canva's templates and customization options to create ads that align with your brand and capture audience attention.

6. Impactful Presentations:
Create compelling presentations that leave a lasting impression. Canva's presentation templates are not only visually appealing but also easy to customize. Incorporate your branding elements to ensure a consistent look throughout your slides.

7. Product Packaging Design:
Design product packaging that stands out on shelves or online platforms. Canva enables you to

create custom labels, tags, or packaging designs. Maintain brand consistency with your chosen color palette, fonts, and logo placement.

8. Branded Merchandise:
Design merchandise such as T-shirts, mugs, or tote bags with Canva. Incorporate your brand elements into the design to create merchandise that serves as both promotional material and an extension of your brand identity.

9. Email Campaign Graphics:
Enhance your email marketing campaigns with visually appealing graphics. Create header images, banners, or promotional graphics using Canva's design tools. Ensure

that your email visuals align with your overall branding strategy.

10. Event Invitations:
Craft stylish and personalized event invitations with Canva. Whether it's for a product launch, webinar, or networking event, design invitations that reflect the tone and style of your brand. Canva's templates make the process efficient and visually impressive.

Practical applications of Canva in designing marketing materials extend across various platforms and formats. With its user-friendly interface and versatile features, Canva empowers businesses to create professional, on-brand marketing collateral that leaves a lasting impact on their target audience.

-6.2 Crafting Professional Presentations

Presentations are a powerful tool for communication, and Canva provides an intuitive platform to craft professional and visually stunning slides. Here's a guide on how to use Canva for creating impactful presentations:

1. Start with a Strong Foundation:
Begin by selecting a presentation template that aligns with your content and style preferences. Canva

offers a variety of professionally designed templates, saving you time and providing a polished starting point.

2. Consistent Branding:
Maintain a consistent brand identity throughout your presentation. Utilize Canva's Brand Kit to incorporate your logo, brand colors, and fonts into the slides. Consistent branding enhances credibility and reinforces your visual identity.

3. Clean and Readable Design:
Opt for a clean and readable design to ensure that your audience can easily follow your content. Choose legible fonts, use appropriate font sizes, and maintain a balanced

layout. Canva's design tools make it easy to achieve a professional and polished look.

4. Visual Hierarchy:

Establish a visual hierarchy to guide your audience through the presentation. Utilize Canva's tools to emphasize key points, create section headers, and use contrasting colors to draw attention to important information. A clear visual hierarchy enhances comprehension.

5. Engaging Visuals:

Incorporate engaging visuals to support your message. Use Canva to create custom graphics, charts, and infographics that illustrate your points effectively. Visuals break up text and keep your audience engaged throughout the presentation.

6. Dynamic Transitions:

Enhance the flow of your presentation with dynamic transitions. Canva provides a range of transition effects between slides, adding a professional touch to your overall presentation. Use transitions strategically to create a seamless and engaging experience.

7. Consistent Image Treatment:

If using images in your presentation, maintain a consistent image treatment. Ensure that images share a similar style, such as color grading or filters, to create a cohesive visual narrative. Canva's image editing tools make this process simple and effective.

8. Smart Use of Icons and Elements: Integrate icons and elements to add visual interest to your slides. Canva's extensive library provides a wide array of icons and elements that can be customized to suit your presentation's theme. Icons and elements help convey concepts visually.

9. Collaborative Editing: Leverage Canva's collaborative features to work seamlessly with team members or clients. Collaborative editing ensures that everyone involved can contribute,

review, and refine the presentation in real time, streamlining the collaborative process.

10. Export Options:
Once your presentation is complete, use Canva's export options to save and share your work. Whether you need a PDF, PowerPoint, or other formats, Canva ensures that your presentation is ready for various platforms and audiences.

Canva's user-friendly interface and versatile design features make it an ideal platform for crafting professional presentations. Whether you're creating business proposals, educational slides, or conference presentations, Canva empowers you to deliver impactful content with a visually appealing and polished design.

www.ingramcontent.com/pod-product-compliance
Lightning Source LLC
Chambersburg PA
CBHW070847310526
45796CB00014B/219